New Dawn Kitchen

Delicious Gluten-free, Vegan,
and Easily Sugar-Free Desserts

Dawn Grey

New Dawn Kitchen
Gluten-free, Vegan, and easily Sugar-Free Desserts
Dawn Grey

Visit our website at **www.newdawnkitchen.com**

Library of Congress Cataloging-in-Publication Data

ISBN-10: 1452824452
ISBN-13: 9781452824451
Printed in the United States of America
Second Edition February 2011

Acknowledgements

This book would not be possible with the contributions of:

Deb and Ashley, for recipe requests, suggestions, and other unlimited support that writers offer to other writers.

My husband, Mark, who was the "behind the scenes" assistant in every way: reliable helper, motivator, and kitchen cleaner-upper. You sampled the good, the bad, and the horrid, dealt with the aftermath of exploding Bundt cakes, and demonstrated your love and loyalty in ways no other man ever could.

To my friends at Unity Church of Lawrence who encouraged me to listen to my heart and ultimately pursue this project.

Finally, Twilight, my feline friend and fellow Yogi. Thank you for your suggestions for this and other books yet to come. I'll keep our conversations just between us.

Table of Contents

Introduction

We have all experienced moments in our lives when we realize our lives have changed forever. These moments define our character and shape our future. I believe it is not what happens to us but how we react to what happens to us that ultimately create our life experience.

While I have had my ups and downs in life like anyone else, from dealing with chronic illness to my lifelong struggle with weight, nothing has impacted my life more than the realization that there are some foods that I cannot eat without severe impact to my health and well-being: dairy, egg yolks, shellfish, and refined and bleached wheat and gluten containing foods. While the omission of shellfish was no big deal, as I have been a vegetarian more on than off since age 17, the impact of losing wheat, gluten, and dairy were immense. I love vegetables and primarily eat vegan anyway, but wheat? What was I to do about bread? Pasta? But most of all, what about my baking?

I am the "go to" girl in my group when it comes to baking. I volunteered to bake at any work occasion, for anyone's party, and especially for holidays. It was discovered early on in my cooking career that I have the knack of duplicating a recipe if I take the time to eat it slowly, examine its texture, and carefully pay attention to its scent, color, and weight. I can even create a recipe by just looking at the finished product, examining the initial recipe, and find ways to make it even better than before. Sure, I could continue to bake, but I am a cook and baker who was trained to sample her finished product before serving it, and now many of those samples would be off-limits.

For those who suffer from Celiac disease, lactose intolerance, or must abstain from any other food due to intolerance or sensitivity (allergies can be serious but often affect people differently than an intolerance) you are all too familiar with stomach pain so bad you feel you have been poisoned, spasms in the GI tract that have you convinced an alien being is about to break out of your body and rip you in half, and/or intestinal issues so severe you promise yourself you will never eat anything ever again, you know what it feels like to deviate from your safe diet. However, you also know what it feels like to be left out, be treated different, and eat bland, boring substitutes for the real thing. I was faced with such a decision on my 30th birthday, and it is a day I never want to relive again. My husband treated me to a lovely surprise dinner party at an Italian restaurant with some of my closest friends, and had a custom cake made especially for me. I knew if I ate a whole piece I would regret it, but just a taste? So, I had two bites, claimed I was full, and thought all was well. How wrong I was. Not only did I feel horrible within an hour, on my birthday with this great party in progress, but I realized that there must be many children who are in my shoes. I was an adult and have had more than my share of birthday cakes. No child should feel torn between being sick and feeling normal. I made a commitment right then and there to learn how to bake and cook meals that were delicious, safe to eat, and good enough that everyone at the table would share it. I did not want that syndrome of having a "special piece of pie". I wanted to be able to have a slice of cake on my birthday, apple pie on Thanksgiving, and a Christmas cookie without hours of distress and time off of work.

Certainly there are many products for sale that are Gluten-free, vegan, and sugar-free, but no store bought item, regardless of how good it is, can substitute for the experience that only your own baking can bring. There is something about the smell of warm cinnamon rolls rising in the oven, their aroma wafting through the kitchen, that cannot be replaced by eating a packaged animal cracker designed for colicky babies.

As a certified holistic health practitioner with a PhD in my field, I have ten years of training in dietary wellness, nutrition, how allergies and intolerances can diminish health, and numerous methods including fasting, detoxification, supplementation, and herbal recipes galore to assist in achieving wholeness and recovery. What my years of training failed to share with me was one single recipe for those who suffer from any of these conditions. The only official remedy I could suggest to my clients was abstinence. That was easy to say when the client was not me. Just as diets do not work because of the limits and deprivation they usually employ, health via abstinence is not always easy, even for those who get immensely sick from a bite of a brownie or those who understand the physiology of Celiac disease and how over time, those few bites can lead to intestinal surgery, ulcers, and malnutrition. What was needed was a plan of action, a viable option so those who needed to abstain from one food category could simply replace it with another, safer option, so they did not feel they were missing out. It was at that moment, while friends were gleefully celebrating my birthday, when my work took a whole new turn. My mission would be to create recipes that were just as delicious, if not better, than the goodies I had been known for. It was on that day, October 4, 2001, that the New Dawn Kitchen officially began.

Many cooking lessons and kitchen experiments later, I devised recipes that I shared with local clients during holistic coaching sessions. Not only were they enjoying the snack samples, but they wanted the recipes themselves. Since there is some real chemistry involved in baking Gluten-free, I had to write out careful instructions of how to use and work with certain flours, starches, and gums. When my clients were no longer sabotaging their gluten/wheat-free diets, they began to really feel and look better. Some lost weight, while others felt as if a whole new chapter of their lives emerged. All of them were excited to get into the kitchen and enjoy baking again. Their children and partners ate them, most without ever suspecting a thing. At the encouragement of friends and clients, I share this book with all of you who need to follow a restricted diet. Yes, you can have your cake and eat it too.

While I must stress that none of my recipes count as health food, and no one should live on crumb cake alone, for those who must abstain from wheat, gluten, dairy, and eggs, these recipes are safe, yummy, and are lot more like the real thing than what you can purchase in a store.

What Exactly is Gluten?

We have all been hearing a lot of talk about gluten, but what exactly is it, you may ask. Gluten is the protein that naturally occurs in many grains: wheat, rye, barley, durum, semolina, einkorn, graham, bulgur wheat, spelt, farro, kamut, and triticale. This gluten is what causing the sticky and chewy texture in our baked goods. For 10% of the population, gluten is simply enemy #1.

Oats are currently under debate as to their gluten content. Commercial oats contain gluten due to cross-contamination in processing, but actually are supposedly Gluten-free otherwise (you can find bags of Gluten-free oats in most natural food markets). Depending on your level of sensitivity will depend if you can use regular oats or if you need to invest in oats that specifically indicate they are Gluten-free. I myself am not sensitive enough for the cross-contamination of oats, so I buy regular oats, which are more affordable and certainly easier to obtain. I would consult with your healthcare provider or nutritionist as to whether or not you can handle oats, or any product for that matter, that is processed on equipment or manufactured in the same environment, as a gluten product.

Therefore, gluten will be present in these grains flours and byproducts, such as barley malt, beer, and many flavorings and spices. When in doubt, obtain vanilla, spices, and any food product that says Gluten-free, as gluten is in many products you may not expect it to be, for example, confectioner's sugar. (I offer you instructions on how to make your own in the sugar-free section.)

Why Eat Wheat/Gluten-free?

There is a growing awareness that a number of individuals experience mild to severe gastro-intestinal distress when eating wheat/gluten containing foods. While most individuals are more likely to have sensitivity to these foods if eaten in excess, there are those who have allergies to wheat or gluten and therefore cannot safely eat even a small portion of the culprit food.

Another concern is Celiac Disease mentioned earlier, which is a condition in which a person is intolerant to gluten containing foods. In the body of someone with this condition, consuming gluten containing food sets off an autoimmune response that causes damage to the small intestine. This, in turn, causes the small intestine to lose the ability to absorb nutrients, leading to malnutrition, permanent intestinal damage, and possibility of requiring surgery.

There is a belief that removing gluten as well as casein, a protein found in dairy, helps children with Autism Spectrum Disorder. Some parents report improvements in autism symptoms with this dietary regimen. Little actual research has been done, however, on the Gluten-free/casein-free diet for autism. However, since there is no dietary need for gluten or casein in the diet, so there is no harm in removing them if they help you or your child's health. Some attribute gluten to complicating or causing other mental health conditions such as depression, schizophrenia, and bipolar disorder. I have personally talked to individuals who insist that it was only upon the removal of all gluten and casein from their diets that they got their sanity back, without the use of medications. Food and mood will be studied more extensively in this century, I assure you, and do expect to hear more and more connections between our food and conditions.

For those who find that eating wheat and/or gluten containing foods creates mild to moderate distress, it is recommended to follow an elimination diet and consult with a healthcare provider and/or dietician for further assistance. In my situation, my gluten and wheat intolerance is limited to refined and bleached grains, mostly spanning the winter months, whereas my egg yolk and dairy allergies are constant. I discovered this by eliminating all wheat, gluten, dairy, eggs, soy, shellfish, nuts, and seeds, and then each week reintroducing each category, one at a time, and evaluated my health and mood. The instant relief, followed by the instant reactions to refined wheat, soy, dairy, egg yolks, and gluten were immediate. I did not need a medical test to confirm what my body was telling me- these are foods that I cannot tolerate in any quantity. I simply eat other foods and bake with other flours quite successfully, and have my health and life back in order.

What Grains and Flours are Gluten-free?

Grains, flours, and starches that are Gluten-free include:

Corn flour, cornmeal, and cornstarch
Buckwheat and buckwheat flour
Rice flour-white and brown
Quinoa, quinoa cereal flakes, and quinoa flour
Millet and millet flour
Sorghum flour
Amaranth and amaranth flour
Certified Gluten-free oats and oatmeal
Coconut flour
Teff flour
Nut meals and flours-almond, chestnut, pecan, cashew
Garbanzo, fava bean, pea, soy and other bean flours
Tapioca pearls and tapioca starch/flour (they are the same product)
Potato starch
Potato flour (which is different than potato starch)
Sweet potato and yam flour
Arrowroot starch

About Gluten-free Flours

Since Gluten-free flours are composed of different ingredients, they will in turn have different textures. This is why it's best to blend and create your own mixes. I have created for myself pre-mixed blends designed for general baking, bread baking, and another for cakes.

Medium weight flours are best to stand in as All-purpose flour. I most frequently use sorghum, garbanzo, and white or brown rice flours, along with one or more starches, to create my own all purpose blend, which I will share later on.

While you are already thinking that this is a whole lot to think of when you get that urge to make a batch of cookies, think again. Once you gather your ingredients, you can blend up mixes in large batches and freeze or refrigerate.

Since there are many flours to work with, your own blend may vary from my personal tastes, and you may find you actually like your finished product better than the original! However, there are many good brands of All-purpose flours already on the market and readily available, such as Bob's Red Mill in most stores, and Jules Gluten-free **www.julesglutenfree.com** available online only at time this second edition went to press (my preferred blend other than my own) that you never really need to worry about mixing your own. In time, you may prefer to blend your own as you gain experience in Gluten-free cooking.

When it comes to any of the starches, you can substitute any of them interchangeably, but you may find that you have a taste preference to one over the other. I prefer cornstarch in desserts only because it is the easiest to find and most affordable, but when making a loaf of bread, I prefer potato or tapioca starch. Guar and Xanthan gums, necessary binding agents for Gluten-free success, are also interchangeable. You may find Guar gum more affordable but a bit harder to find. Online searches should yield you many sources, such as Barry Farms.

Please note as you proceed with these or your own recipes that you may have to adjust the moisture level in my recipes if you use different flours than I have used or if you live at a higher altitude. I am in the flatlands of Kansas, so higher altitude residents may need to fine tune things. You also need a good sense of humor to begin your Gluten-free adventure, as it appears that the right balance of flours, gum, and leavening are essential. My first attempt at a Bundt cake rendered an explosion in the oven, with half of the cake remaining in the pan looking like an uncooked piece of French toast, and the part that exploded was as crispy as a sugar cone.

One other detail I discovered is that most Gluten-free recipes need to have the oven on average of 25 degrees cooler than the original. I cannot tell you how many raw yet blackened cookies I went through before I figured this out. However, ovens vary, so try one batch first, and see what you yield.

New Dawn Kitchen's Gluten-Free All-Purpose Blend
(Makes 6 cups)

2 cups sorghum flour
1 cup garbanzo flour
½ cup coconut flour or almond meal flour
½ cup Gluten-free oat or quinoa flour
1 cup cornstarch
1 cup tapioca starch/flour

Dairy Products: To Eat or Not to Eat

While most of us are familiar with lactose intolerance and milk allergies, there are other reasons why more and more individuals are reducing or eliminating dairy from their diets. In this age of environmental awareness, using a plant-based milk substitute is more and more popular as of late due to its smaller impact on environmental waste.

Also, for those who are concerned about animal cruelty, avoiding milk helps reduce factory farming practices. Since most dairy cows are supplied with antibiotics, hormones, and fed food that is laced with pesticides, it may be best if we all took a step away from dairy.

For those of you who are vegan (choose to eliminate all animal products), dairy allergic, or lactose intolerant, follow the recipes using whatever milk substitute you wish. You will also find that many of the recipes call for yogurt and/or sour cream. For convenience I will call these "milk product", "vegan sour cream", and "non-dairy yogurt " the first time, and from there, just yogurt, milk, etc. If you bought this book because of your gluten/wheat sensitivity and are not following a dairy free guideline, feel free to use whatever dairy products you wish in equal measure, but I do suggest you try them with non-dairy items just once, to see that those who choose to use dairy alternatives are by no means suffering.

Fats: The Good, the Bad, and the Ugly

Remember when margarine first came out and we thought it was healthful to smear gobs of it on our food to get the healthful polyunsaturated fats? Well, like most other food trends, the good and the bad fats list keeps getting updated. Here is my take on fats, as far as this cookbook is concerned: use what is readily available to you. While I am the first to say no to traditional shortening, if you prefer it, then use it. However, please be sure it is a vegan shortening, and dairy-free if it is butter flavored. While I did my best to be conscious of the amount of fat, salt, and sugar, included, these are not health foods.

Consuming too many fats, even the healthful ones, can increase your calorie intake and weight. My cinnamon roll recipe, for example, should not be seen as a healthful breakfast instead of oatmeal, nor do I want you to stuff yourself with banana bread or carrot cake to obtain their vitamins. However, I am the first to say that I love a good treat, and unless advised otherwise by a healthcare provider, a Gluten-free vegan cinnamon roll in moderation every now and then should not derail your weight loss goals or healthy lifestyle. Just use common sense.

However, the main fat most of us need to substitute in dairy-free and vegan baking is butter. Butter in many ways may actually be healthier than the trans fats in most margarines and shortenings, but for those who cannot or will not have dairy, both products are likely unsafe to use. My suggestion for recipes that really need a "stick" of butter is to use vegan brands such as "Earth Balance". It took some initial getting used to when I first developed my dairy sensitivity, but now I prefer its taste to the original. They make a regular and a soy-free, and it is for sale at most major grocers.

My recommended and preferred fat of choice for cakes, brownies, and just about any other baking is coconut oil. It is solid at room temperature and requires heat to melt into liquid. If you choose to use coconut oil, measure it after it has melted for liquid oil substitution, and solid, like you would measure shortening, for replacing butter or shortening.

Coconut oil is reported to have numerous health benefits, including replenishing the thyroid, antiseptic and antibiotic properties, and even weight loss benefits as it will be burned before any other dietary fat for energy. Some brands are pricier than others, but I have learned that the higher the price, the better the flavor. The lower priced ones in general smell and taste like coconut, so keep this in mind, but the more expensive brands yield a buttery flavor that is untouched even by the creamiest butter. I like to use it when a mild coconut flavor, should it come through, would only enhance the food's flavor. Keep in mind that even lower cost coconut oil can be more than seven dollars for a jar that is smaller than a jar of spaghetti sauce, and you might wind up using the whole thing, if not more, for one recipe. Therefore when I bake cakes and recipes that require a lot of oil, I rely on canola oil. If you prefer another oil besides canola, simply substitute that oil for the butter or oil called for in a recipe. I do not recommend olive oil, as it is too strong, and is reported to be carcinogenic when heated to high temperatures, so it is best for salad dressings.

Egg-Free Baking

If you are vegan or cannot consume eggs like me, you have several options to use as substitutes. Unlike swapping oils and milk for another product, not every egg substitute will work for every recipe, so removing eggs from a recipe is perhaps just as tricky, if not more so, than making the Gluten-free switch. My experience is that if you have a recipe that requires whipping eggs or egg whites to make the recipe what it is, say soufflé or meringue, you may want to (temporarily) say good bye to those until new products emerge. There is currently no egg substitute that is vegan and can mimic an omelet, though much can be said for scrambled tofu. The type of egg replacing we need is for baking, and it can be done if you take the time to experiment with which product mimics the best texture for your recipe. Most of my recipes will use a product called Ener-G Egg Replacer, which I refer to as Egg Replacer, as well as applesauce, fruit puree, flaxseed meal, and mashed tofu. There is a balance between the wetness of a fruit puree or tofu and the dryness of a powder mixed in water, so you will learn by trial and error which type of replacer to use, and what other modifications may be needed in the recipe to yield the best results.

Need to Reduce Fat?

While our recipes will be naturally cholesterol-free because we have omitted all animal products, almost all of our recipes contain oil, vegan margarine, or both. Most of these recipes as they are presented are not low-fat. There is however, much that can be done about this.

For those who need or want to reduce the fat, there are a number of substitutions you can use. One of the most popular is to use applesauce. Unsweetened applesauce works well in recipes, as does pumpkin, mashed sweet potato, or any Gluten-free pureed fruit or baby food. If you are already using one of these for your egg replacement, be careful not to add too much, or your recipe will be too wet. My suggestion is to use a puree or any fruit for up to 50% of the fat content. To use more will either yield a very dry or overly wet product. I also suggest flax or Egg Replacer powder for the egg replacement as well as potentially reducing any other liquid in the recipe.

Want to Reduce Sugar?

You have the choice in just about every single recipe here whether you will use natural or artificial sweeteners. In standard baking recipes, ¾ cup liquid sweeteners, such as agave nectar, maple syrup, or rice syrup, will work fine (remember barley malt is not Gluten-free and honey is not vegan). Reduce liquid in recipe by ¼ cup. If your recipe does not call for liquid to reduce, I would consider a granulated sweetener instead. I am very sugar sensitive, so for my own baking, I use artificial sweetener and/or sugar-free maple syrup. While artificial sweeteners are not healthful in the least, this is one of those choices I need to make if I want to eat sweets, and I know that there is no such thing as a truly "healthy" cupcake anyway, so it comes down to moderation. While maple syrup, rice syrup, and agave nectar are more healthful choices than refined white sugar, they still have a sugar content that spike my blood sugar if I have more than a couple of bites.

When you see instructions for granulated sweetener, you can use any granulated, whether traditional sugar, evaporated cane crystals, or even Splenda®, Nutrasweet®, Xylitol, or Stevia. There are white and brown artificial sweeteners, and you can use these in equal measure for what is called for in my recipes.

Confectioner's sugar is not only **not** vegan (traditional white sugar is bleached and processed with animal bones) but it can contain gluten, depending on the manufacturer. I never would have thought of it until I made a batch of frosting, and got horribly sick after a few too many taste tests. While I am sure there are Gluten-free varieties available, *you can make your own confectioner's sugar by blending your granulated sweetener of choice with a bit of cornstarch until you get the right consistency.* My suggestion, as the measurements vary greatly depending on the sweetening product, is use 1 Tablespoon of any starch of choice (to start) with ½ cup granulated sweetener. Keep adding starch until you get a texture to the fine, powdery one that confectioner's sugar is. I like to do this blending in a coffee grinder in small batches and make it fresh, just before I need it.

When you see instructions for liquid sweetener, again, please use what works best for you. You can use rice syrup, agave nectar, real maple syrup, sugar-free maple syrup, or any other you encounter that is Gluten-free, vegan, and if needed, sugar-free. Use these in equal measure for what is called for in my recipes.

Ultimately the choice is yours when it comes to sweetening your goods. Remember when using a liquid sweetener, use less than the amount of sugar called for unless my recipe already calls for a liquid sweetener (taste test to adjust sweetness level). Adjust the liquid by two Tablespoons less to begin with.

Substitutes for Cream and Condensed Milk Products

Recently I discovered a groovy product named Mimic Cream that works for those of us who need a Gluten-free vegan cream product. It is on the grocery shelf in one of those aseptic containers that soymilk comes in, and does not require refrigeration after opening. I make the most awesome Italian food, Indian food, and just about all other food with this (but these recipes appear in my other vegan and Gluten-free cookbooks). It can also work wonders with coffee and blended drinks.

To make your own non-dairy condensed milk

If you are like me, you prefer to make your own processed foods so you can control what is in it and always have it on hand. It is also considerably cheaper in almost every instance to make your own. Making your own condensed, non-dairy milk is quite easy, and once I figured out how, I realized how foolish I was in avoiding recipes containing them. All you need is:

3 cups non-dairy milk

½ cup granulated sweetener of choice

Stir ingredients together in a sauce pan and heat gently; cook slowly over low to almost medium heat, stirring constantly, until the volume is reduced to about 1 cup. Add some vanilla extract to taste, if you like; and a pinch of sea salt, if desired. Cool the condensed milk and refrigerate if not using right away.

For Evaporated Coconut or Non-Dairy Milk

Follow directions as in the previous recipe, but omit the sugar and pour the milk into a saucepan; cook gently over low to medium heat, stirring until the coconut milk is thickened and reduced to 1½ cups. Cool. Refrigerate.

Peanut-Free/Nut-Free

For a nut-free peanut butter substitute try using sunflower seed butter, commonly found as the product "Sunbutter" in recipes. You can also make your own pumpkin seed butter. Sesame seed butter (also called tahini) is another choice, but requires (in my opinion) a touch of liquid sweetener and a pinch of salt to offset its savory taste. Other seed and nut butters include macadamia nut butter, cashew butter, pecan butter, and my favorite, almond butter. You may want to sweeten or salt the recipe differently depending on your like for salt and sweet. If you can tolerate soy, soynut butter is readily available and being marketed as a "safe school alternative" as some school districts are banning peanut butter inside the classroom due to their severe allergic reactions to some children.

Salt-Free

There are a number of potassium salt products out there for those who must watch their sodium intake. All are fine, but please do not use an herbal blend like Mrs. Dash® for baking! Potassium salt seems more salty and concentrated than regular salt, so you might want to go lighter on it when using it in baking.

Soy-Free

Now that soy is becoming a mainstream product and additive in countless items, we are seeing more and more instances of soy allergies and intolerances. For those who have Hypothyroidism, Perimenopause, or other hormonal issues, you may be asked to reduce or remove soy from your diet. Soy has goitergens, which attack the thyroid, and can create thyroid issues if consumed in large quantities. In fact, I developed soy-induced Hypothyroidism because I went soy crazy. I used soymilk, soy yogurt, soy, soy, soy. Then one day, I woke up, and the outer third of my eyebrows were simply gone. I panicked and thought this was the horrific side effect of radiation exposure, but an online search indicated it was a classic sign of Hypothyroidism (low thyroid function). Once I severely restricted my soy, my condition literally corrected itself in weeks. My eyebrows began to grow back in, my body temperature increased (no more cold hands and feet), migraines that I had 2 or 3 times a week went away, and some weight gain that I attributed to testing one too many recipes melted off. All this without any medication, traditional or herbal, for Hypothyroidism.

If you need to avoid soy, I recommend using rice milk, rice vegan cheese, Daiya brand Gluten-free vegan cheeses, soy-free Earth Balance vegan butter, and substitute rice milk powder, and rice protein whenever you see soy. In most cases, mashed tofu can be replaced with unsweetened applesauce or other fruit puree in recipes.

Final Comments

My experience is that many Gluten-free batters and doughs are not as yummy as their wheat counterparts, so please do not throw out the cake because the batter tastes icky. Their texture may seem gummier, but the finished product, if mixed correctly, will be great. So, you will not lick the bowl or have raw cookie dough like you used to, but what is more important- a real cookie or a lick of a bowl?

Read through each recipe and make sure you have the ingredients on hand. It is hard to substitute Gluten-free vegan, at least at first, and 1 cup of corn flour may not yield the same results as a cup of All-purpose Gluten-free flour. Make sure you like the taste of your sweetener before deciding to use a cup of it in your recipe. Often, complain Gluten-free baking is hard or terrible, but it is simply a process of patience and discovery, and once you find the right fat, flour, sweetener, and milk, you will be amazed at how delicious the results are.

Breakfast Goodies

Fruit Filled Danishes

I had never been a fan of Danishes before I developed this recipe for one of my new celiac clients, who just could not have hermorning coffee without a Danish. In my opinion, these are better than the original.

Makes 2 dozen

Danish Ingredients
¼ cup coconut oil, margarine, or vegan shortening
½ cup sugar-free maple syrup or other liquid sweetener
Egg Replacer for 2 eggs, prepared according to instructions
2 Tablespoons active dry yeast
1 container vegan sour cream
½ cup cornstarch
1½ cups Gluten-free All-purpose flour
½ teaspoon baking soda
2 teaspoons baking powder
2 teaspoons Xanthan or Guar gum
1 teaspoon salt
1 teaspoon apple cider vinegar
For Topping
Fruit jam or pie filling of choice

Preheat oven to 350°F.
Combine all Danish ingredients, stirring well to remove any lumps. Make individual Danishes by placing ¼ cup dough on a greased baking sheet. Use a glass or biscuit cutter to mold into a flat round. Make a small dent in the middle of the Danish with a spoon for the filling. Continue until all dough is used. Place 1 Tablespoon of filling in the middle of each Danish.

Bake for 15 minutes, rotating cookie sheets once after 8 minutes.

Cranberry Orange Scones

This is one of the few recipes where I prefer oat flour to an All-purpose blend for its added nutrients, but you can substitute your favorite All-purpose blend of choice. This recipe can be halved, but I prefer to make the full amount and freeze any leftovers.

Makes 2 dozen

8 cups Gluten-free oat flour or Gluten-free All-purpose flour
4 Tablespoons baking powder
2 teaspoons salt
1½ cups oil
2 cups granulated sweetener
4 Tablespoons vanilla
1 cup orange juice, preferably fresh squeezed
4 cups of cranberries, fresh or frozen and thawed
2 teaspoons Xanthan or Guar gum

Preheat oven to 350°F.

Grease 2 cookie sheets. Mix together all dry ingredients, then add in all liquid ingredients. Batter will be thick and somewhat dry compared to a muffin batter. Use a Tablespoon or small scoop to portion out scones equally among the two pans. Use non-stick spray or a light brushing of oil to coat the top of each one.

Bake scones for 10 minutes, rotate pans, and bake another 5-10 minutes, or until the scones are golden and firm.

Blueberry Muffins

Feel free to substitute raspberries, strawberries, or any mixed fruit.

Makes 2 dozen

4 cups Gluten-free All-purpose flour
4 teaspoons baking powder
4 teaspoons baking soda
2 teaspoons of Xanthan or Guar gum
2 teaspoons salt
½ cup unsweetened applesauce
1 cup oil
2 cups granulated sweetener
1½ cups milk product
4 Tablespoons vanilla
1 ½ cups fresh or thawed blueberries
1 teaspoon lemon extract

Preheat oven to 350°F.

Fill muffin tins with liners. Stir together all dry ingredients. Next, add the applesauce, oil, sugar, milk, and vanilla. Gently fold in the blueberries, just enough to mix into the batter without breaking them.

Fill each cup about halfway with batter, roughly 1/3 cup each. Bake on center rack for 15 minutes, rotate, and bake another 10 minutes or until a toothpick comes out clean.

Cinnamon Rolls

Breads of any kind were a challenge for me, as I while I was a great cookie and cake baker, I had limited experience with any type of dough. Something about having to use a rolling pin would set me into a spin. However, with a little work, I managed to get this recipe just right.

Makes 1 dozen

Dough
4 teaspoons active dry yeast
1 teaspoon granulated sweetener
1 cup warm water
1 cup milk product
1 teaspoon granulated sweetener
2/3 cup vegan butter
2 teaspoons salt
3 cups Gluten-free oat flour
1 cup corn flour
¼ teaspoon baking soda
2 teaspoons baking powder
2 teaspoons Xanthan or Guar gum

Filling
½ cup vegan butter, melted
1/3 cup granulated sweetener
3 Tablespoons cinnamon
¼ cup brown granulated sweetener, regular or sugar-free

Frosting
¼ cup confectioner's sugar
2 teaspoons milk product

Pan Sauce
½ cup vegan butter, melted
1/3 cup granulated sweetener
2 Tablespoons maple syrup

To make the dough

Mix together the yeast with 1 cup warm water and the teaspoon sugar. Set aside. In another bowl mix together the oat and corn flour, baking soda, baking powder and gum. Add yeast mixture to the flour. Add in the milk and salt. Mix thoroughly until dough begins to form.

Knead the dough for several minutes, or use a Kitchen Aid or other Bread Machine that can knead the dough for you. Once dough has been kneaded, place on a floured surface and cover with a warm towel for 1 hour. After the dough has risen, roll out to approximately 16×20 rectangle.

To make the filling

Mix the brown and white sugars together with the cinnamon. Sprinkle evenly over the rolled out rectangle. Next pour the vegan butter on top of the dough. Roll the dough up slowly, while trying not to push any of the filling out. Once rolled, slice into 12 pieces.

For the pan sauce

Pour in the melted butter into a rectangular casserole dish. Next pour in the sugar and then finally spread the maple syrup evenly around. Place each of the 12 pieces inside this dish. Bake inside oven for 45 minutes or until the cinnamon buns look golden brown.

For the frosting

Place the icing sugar and milk into a tiny bowl, mix thoroughly and pour on top of cinnamon bun of choice.

Banana Bread

Makes 2 loaves

2 cups Gluten-free all purpose flour, or 1 cup each
2 teaspoons baking powder
2 teaspoons baking soda
1 teaspoon Xanthan or Guar gum
1 teaspoon cinnamon
½ cup oil
1 cup granulated sweetener
2/3 cup milk product
½ cup unsweetened applesauce
1 ½ cups mashed overripe bananas
1 Tablespoon vanilla
1 Tablespoon peanut butter or other nut butter
½ teaspoon of salt
½ cup chopped nuts, vegan chocolate chips, or raisins, optional

Preheat oven to 350°F.

Grease 2 bread loaves. Blend together all dry ingredients. Add all wet ingredients one at a time, except the bananas, until smooth. Finally add bananas until well incorporated. Divide batter equally between the two pans.

Bake 20 minutes, rotate pans, and bake another 20 minutes until a toothpick comes out clean.

Apple Fritters

Makes 1 dozen

4 large apples (I use Fuji or Macintosh)
1 cup Gluten-free All-purpose flour
1½ teaspoons baking powder
1 ½ cups milk product
4 Tablespoons sugar
1 teaspoon cinnamon
A pinch of salt
2 Tablespoons lemon juice
4 cups cold water
1 ½ cups or more of oil, for frying
¼ cup sifted confectioner's sugar

In a bowl mix together flour, sugar, baking powder, cinnamon, and salt. Slice apples, removing skins if desired. Add to the flour mix. Add milk to the dry ingredients.

Prepare your deep fryer or frying pan, heating oil under a drop of batter splatters on contact. Don't overload the pan or else the oil temperature will drop too quickly, only one layer at a time. Fry about 1 ½ -2 minutes each side until a beautiful golden brown. Take them out using a slotted metal spoon or spatula and place single file on the paper towels.

When done, sprinkle with confectioner's sugar, or optional glaze.

Donut Holes

Egg Replacer for two eggs, prepared according to package
1 cup granulated sweetener
2 Tablespoons canola oil
¾ cup milk product
1 teaspoon apple cider vinegar
3 ½ cups all purpose Gluten-free flour blend
3 teaspoons Xanthan or Guar gum
2 teaspoons baking powder
1 teaspoon baking soda
½ teaspoon salt
½ teaspoon cinnamon
Oil for deep frying
Extra sweetener with 1 teaspoon of cinnamon for coating holes

Stir vinegar into milk to create a buttermilk substitute. Let sit 15 minutes before adding other ingredients. When ready, stir in Egg Replacer, then add sweetener and oil, then mix together and add all remaining dry ingredients, except the sugar and cinnamon set aside for coating. Stir until you have a dough. Sift together sugar and cinnamon, and place in a lunch sized brown paper bag or plastic bag.

Prepare skillet or deep fryer, heating oil to 375°F or heat oil until a drop of water creates splattering. Drop rounded Tablespoons of batter, about 6 at a time, into fryer or pan so as to maintain the temperature of oil. Cook 1-3 minutes, or until light golden brown. While they are still warm, shake them in the paper bag with cinnamon sweetener mix.

Corn Bread

Makes 2 loaves

1½ cups up Gluten-free All-purpose flour
1 cup cornmeal
1 cup corn flour
4 teaspoons baking powder
2 teaspoons baking soda
2 teaspoons salt
2 teaspoons Xanthan or Guar gum
1 can creamed corn (yes, this is dairy-free)
2/3 cup liquid sweetener (I prefer agave in this one)
½ cup oil
4 teaspoons of vanilla
1 cup milk product
2 Tablespoons apple cider vinegar
1 cup shredded vegan cheese, optional

Preheat oven to 350°F.

Create a buttermilk substitute by combining the vinegar with the milk. Set aside while preparing the rest of the ingredients, except the cheese if using.

In a large bowl, combine all of the dry ingredients. Add the corn, oil, sweetener, and vanilla. Stir well. Stir in the buttermilk. Blend well.

Equally divide batter amongst the two pans. Bake 30 minutes, rotate the pans, add the cheese to the top of the pans if using, and bake another 20 minutes, or until a toothpick comes out clean.

Chocolate Donut Holes

I really adore these and they are great for children's parties.

1 cup brown rice flour
2/3 cup cornstarch
1/3 cup tapioca flour
¼ cup cocoa powder
2 teaspoons baking powder
1 teaspoon baking soda
½ teaspoon salt
1 ½ teaspoons Xanthan or Guar gum
1 cup granulated sweetener
¼ cup vegan sour cream
Egg Replacer for 2 eggs, prepared according to package
¾ cup plain milk product with 2 teaspoons of cider vinegar added
2 Tablespoons vegan margarine, shortening, or coconut oil
Oil for skillet or deep fryer

Mix all ingredients. Refrigerate at least 2 hours.

Preheat deep fryer to 375°F or heat enough oil in heavy skillet to submerge dough in oil.

Drop teaspoonfuls of batter into oil. Fry 1-3 minutes or until they are puffy.

Drain on a thick layer of paper towels.

Zucchini Bread

The first time I had zucchini bread, I thought it was awesome. Then I learned how much fat it has. This version has about half of the fat of most regular zucchini bread recipes. You can even make this using yellow squash instead if you prefer.

Makes 2 loaves

3 cups Gluten-free oat or All-purpose flour
1 cup tapioca starch
½ cup flaxseed meal
2 teaspoons baking powder
2 teaspoons baking soda
1 teaspoon salt
2 teaspoons vanilla extract
1 cup granulated sweetener
1 cup plain milk product
¼ cup oil
½ cup unsweetened applesauce
2 cups shredded zucchini
1 teaspoon Xanthan or Guar gum

Preheat oven to 350° F.

Grease two bread loaf pans. Blend flour, starch, gum, salt, baking powder, baking soda, and flaxseed meal. Next add oil, applesauce, sugar, milk, vanilla, and mix gently. Do not over stir. Finally, fold in the zucchini.

Divide batter equally among the two pans. Bake 30 minutes, rotate, and bake about 10-15 minutes or until toothpick comes out clean.

Lemon Blueberry Coffee Cake

1 cup softened vegan margarine
1 cup granulated sweetener
Egg Replacer for 3 eggs, prepared according to instructions
½ cup liquid sweetener
1 cup non-dairy yogurt, lemon or blueberry flavored
preferred
1 teaspoon vanilla extract
Zest of two medium lemons
Juice of one lemon
2½ cups gluten-free all-purpose flour
1 teaspoon Xanthan or Guar gum
2½ teaspoons baking powder
1 teaspoon baking soda
¼ teaspoon salt
2 cups fresh blueberries
Topping
1 cup chopped pecans
½ cup granulated sweetener
1 teaspoon cinnamon

Preheat oven to 350°F.
Cream together butter and sweetener. Add prepared Egg Replacer.

In another bowl, mix yogurt, vanilla, lemon zest and lemon juice.
Combine flour, gum, baking powder, soda, and salt. Add flour and
yogurt to sweetener mixture. Stir in blueberries. Batter may be heavy
and somewhat stiff. Spread half of the batter in a greased 9x13
baking pan. Combine topping ingredients, and sprinkle half of
topping mixture over dough. Carefully spread remaining batter on
top of topping. Sprinkle with remainder of topping.
Bake for 35-40 minutes, or until toothpick comes out clean.

Cakes
and
Cupcakes

New York Style Heavy Crumb Cake

This has been, and likely always will be, my signature recipe.

¼ cup oil
4 cups Gluten-free All-purpose flour
½ cup granulated sweetener
2 teaspoons baking powder
2 teaspoons baking soda
½ teaspoon salt
Egg Replacer for one egg, prepared according to package
½ cup plain milk product
2 teaspoons vanilla
1 cup brown granulated sweetener
1½ teaspoons ground cinnamon
1 cup vegan butter, melted and cooled
2 teaspoons Xanthan or Guar gum
Confectioners' sugar, for dusting

Place rack in center of oven, and preheat oven to 325°F. Grease a 9 x13 baking pan and set aside.

In a medium bowl, sift together 1½ cups flour, granulated sweetener, gum, baking powder and soda, and salt; set aside.

In a second bowl, whisk together the prepared Egg Replacer, milk, oil, and vanilla. Fold dry ingredients into egg mixture. Spread batter evenly into prepared pan, and bake for 20 minutes.

In a medium bowl, combine remaining 2½ cups flour, brown sweetener, and cinnamon. Pour melted butter over flour mixture, and toss with a rubber spatula until large crumbs form. Sprinkle crumbs over batter and bake 20 minutes. Rotate pan and continue baking until a cake tester comes out clean, about 30 minutes more.

Red Velvet Cake

Red Velvet is a beautiful red colored, chocolate flavored cake and is pictured on the book's cover.

2¾ cups Gluten-free All-purpose flour
¼ cup cocoa powder
¾ teaspoon Xanthan gum
1½ teaspoons baking powder
1½ teaspoons baking soda
1½ teaspoons salt
1½ cups milk product
1½ teaspoons cider vinegar
¾ cup vegan butter or shortening
1½ cups granulated sweetener
4½ teaspoons Egg Replacer
6 Tablespoons plain milk product
2 teaspoons vanilla extract
1 bottle red food coloring

Preheat the oven to 350°F. Grease two 8 inch round cake pans, and dust with a little cocoa powder.

Whisk together the flour, cocoa powder, gum, baking powder, baking soda, and salt. Set aside. Make Egg Replacer with the 6 Tablespoons of milk product and set aside.

Combine the milk and vinegar. Set aside. Combine the shortening, sugar, prepared Egg Replacer, and vanilla. Using an electric mixer, beat on medium speed until light and fluffy, about 2-3 minutes. Add the food coloring. Stir in the flour.

Divide the batter equally between the two pans. Bake for about 30-35 minutes, or until toothpick comes out clean. Rotate the pans halfway through the baking time. Frost once cakes have cooled completely.

White Frosting

This is what I used on the Red Velvet cake on the cover, but feel free to us any frosting of your choice. See lemon frosting on page 42 and other options on page 43 for ideas.

2 cups vegan butter or shortening
Pinch of salt
6 cups confectioners' sugar
1/3 cup milk product
2 Tablespoons lemon juice
1 Tablespoon vanilla extract

Cream the butter or shortening with the confectioners' sugar slowly.

Add the milk, lemon juice, and vanilla. Beat on medium speed until creamy.

Frost generously on cake when it is fully cooled.

Lemon Cake

1¾ cups Gluten-free All-Purpose flour
1 teaspoon baking powder
1 teaspoon baking soda
½ teaspoon salt
1 large lemon
½ cup melted vegan margarine
1 cup brown sweetener
Egg Replacer for 2 eggs, prepared according to package
2/3 cup plain milk product
½ teaspoon vanilla
¼ cup confectioner's sugar

Preheat oven to 350°F.

Mix dry ingredients (except sugars). Grate lemon peel and stir in.
Squeeze the lemon juice into a small bowl, mix it with the powdered
sugar, and set it
aside. Beat margarine and brown sugar and add prepared Egg
Replacer. Add flour mixture and milk to margarine mixture. Add
vanilla. Pour into greased 13x9 pan and bake for 30 minutes or until
a toothpick comes out clean.

In a large bowl combine confectioner's sugar and salt. Using a whisk
or electric mixer attachment, add boiling water and whip at low
speed until smooth. Add coconut oil or shortening and margarine to
the sweetener mixture and whip at medium speed approximately 3
minutes. Add vanilla. For best results beat on medium high until it
fluffs up to almost fill the bowl.

Frostings

Lemon Frosting
6 cups confectioner's sugar
½ teaspoon salt
½ cup boiling water
2½ cups Coconut oil at room temperature
1½ sticks vegan butter, cut in small pieces
2 Tablespoons lemon extract

In a large bowl combine confectioner's sugar and salt. Using a whisk or electric mixer, add boiling water and whip (at low speed) until smooth. Add coconut oil and butter to the sweetener mixture and whip at medium speed for approximately 3 minutes. Add vanilla. For best results beat on medium-high until it fluffs up to almost fill the bowl.

Chocolate Frosting
4½ cups confectioner's sugar
1½ cups powdered cocoa
½ teaspoon salt product
½ cup boiling water
2½ cups vegan shortening
1½ sticks vegan butter, cut in small pieces
2 Tablespoon vanilla extract

In a large bowl combine confectioner's sugar and salt. Using a whisk or electric mixer, add boiling water and whip (at low speed) until smooth. Add coconut oil or shortening and margarine to the sweetener mixture and whip at medium speed for approximately 3 minutes. Add vanilla. For best results beat on medium-high until it fluffs up to almost fill the bowl.

Orange Cream Frosting

6 cups confectioner's sugar
½ teaspoon salt product
½ cup orange juice
2½ cups vegan shortening or coconut oil
1½ sticks vegan butter, cut in small pieces
1 Tablespoon orange extract
½ teaspoon grated orange peel

In a large bowl combine confectioner's sugar and salt. Using a whisk or electric mixer, add orange juice and whip at low speed until smooth. Add coconut oil or shortening and butter to the sweetener mixture and whip at medium speed for approximately 3 minutes. Add orange extract. For best results beat on medium-high until I fluffs up to almost fill the bowl.

Chocolate Pound Cake

This cake is especially moist if you keep it frozen and defrost as needed.

2¼ cups Gluten-free All-purpose flour
½ cup cocoa powder
1 teaspoon baking powder
1 teaspoon of baking soda
¼ teaspoon salt
1½ cups vegan butter
2 ¼ cups granulated sweetener
3 Tablespoons Egg Replacer
¾ cup water
1 cup chocolate flavored milk product
2 teaspoons vanilla extract
¾ cup (6 ounce cup) vegan yogurt, vanilla or chocolate flavored

Preheat oven to 325°F. Grease a Bundt pan and set aside.
In a small bowl, combine the Egg Replacer and water and set aside.

In another small bowl, sift together the flour, cocoa powder, baking powder, soda, and salt.

In a medium-sized bowl, cream the butter and 1¾ cups of the sweetener. Add the Egg Replacer mixture at little at a time to the creamed butter and sweetener, mixing well.

Add the flour mixture, alternating with the milk. Once the flour and milk have been combined, add the yogurt and vanilla. Stir well.

Pour batter into prepared pan. Bake for 75 minutes or until toothpick comes out clean.

Chocolate Chip Cupcakes

These are great plain or frosted.

Makes 2 dozen

2½ cups granulated sweetener
3½ cups Gluten-free All-purpose flour
1½ cups vegan margarine or shortening, at room
temperature   1 teaspoon salt
2 cups plain milk product
2 cups vegan chocolate chips
1 Tablespoon Xanthan or Guar gum
2 Tablespoons vanilla extract

Preheat oven to 350° F. Line 2 cupcake pans with liners.

Cream butter in a large bowl, then add all dry ingredients, blending well.

Add chocolate chips. Finally add all liquid ingredients. Pour 1/3 cup batter into each cupcake liner.

Bake 20 minutes, rotating tins at 10 minutes, and continue until toothpick comes out clean.

Let cool 30 minutes before topping with frosting of choice.

Chocolate Cupcakes

The first time I made these, my husband's family came over and ate these unfrosted while I was still sleeping. They never noticed there was anything different about them, and ultimately, that is why I wrote this cookbook.

Makes 2 dozen

2 cups garbanzo flour
½ cup cornstarch
1 cup cocoa powder
1 Tablespoon baking powder
1 Tablespoon baking soda
½ teaspoon Xanthan or Guar gum
2 teaspoons salt
2½ cups granulated sweetener
¾ cup oil
¼ cup applesauce, preferably unsweetened
¾ cup (6 oz) soy yogurt, any flavor
3 Tablespoons vanilla extract
¾ cup milk product
1 cup hot water

Preheat oven to 350° F. Prepare 2 cupcake tins by adding liners.

Mix flour, starch, cocoa, baking soda, baking powder, salt, and gum. Next add oil, sweetener, applesauce, yogurt, and vanilla. Stir well.

Pour boiling water over mixture and mix rapidly for about 30 seconds. Lastly, add the milk and stir until smooth. Pour 1/3 cup of batter into each liner.

Bake 15 minutes, rotate the pans, and then bake another 10-15 minutes, or until toothpick comes out clean.

Marble Cheesecake

1½ cups Graham crumbs from our recipe, page
5 Tablespoons vegan butter or coconut oil
¼ cup cocoa powder
¼ cup white rice flour
2 Tablespoons cornstarch
Cheesecake
1 cup vegan cream cheese
2 Tablespoons of unsweetened applesauce
Egg Replacer for one egg, prepared according to package
2 teaspoons vanilla
½ cup granulated sweetener
8 ounces vegan cream cheese
Egg Replacer for one egg, prepared according to package
½ cup granulated sweetener
¼ cup cocoa powder
1 teaspoon vanilla
1 cup vegan chocolate chips or chocolate pieces

Preheat oven to 350°F. Lightly grease a spring form pan.

Prepare crust by mixing crumbs with flour, cocoa, and starch. Cream in the butter.

Press crumbs into bottom and sides of pan. Bake for 10 minutes, then remove and place in freezer.

Beat cream cheese, sweetener, prepared egg replacer, and vanilla until smooth.

Make the filling by beating the cream cheese, sweetener, prepared Egg Replacer, cocoa, and vanilla until smooth.

50

Add the chips and stir well. Place alternating spoonfuls of chocolate and filling over crust until empty. Gently swirl the two together with a knife to marble.

Bake for 45-50 minutes, or until toothpick inserted comes out clean. Let cool. Cover and refrigerate overnight.

Carrot Cake

A great looking cake for an elaborate gathering.

1 cup brown rice flour
½ cup quinoa or Gluten-free oat flour
2 teaspoons baking powder
1 teaspoon baking soda
1½ teaspoons ground cinnamon
½ teaspoon salt
1 teaspoon Xanthan or Guar gum
½ cup oil
1 cup brown granulated sweetener
1½ teaspoons Egg Replacer, prepared according to package
½ cup unsweetened applesauce
1½ teaspoons vanilla
1½ cups grated carrot
¾ cup crushed pineapple, drained

Preheat oven to 350°F. Lightly coat 9 x 13 inch cake pan with non-stick spray.

Stir together the flours, baking powder and soda, spices, salt, and gum in a medium bowl.

In a large mixing bowl, beat the oil and sugar on high for a few minutes or until thick and creamy. Add the Egg Replacer, applesauce, and vanilla, and stir well. Stir in the carrots and pineapple. Add the dry mixture into the wet mixture and stir.

Pour the batter into the prepared baking dish and bake 30-35 minutes, or until toothpick comes out clean. Cool on a wire rack, and frost with our vegan cream cheese frosting, if desired.

Vegan Cream Cheese Frosting

I use this for most of my cakes, not just carrot cake.

1 cup vegan cream cheese
½ vegan butter
2 cups confectioner's sugar
1 teaspoon vanilla extract
1½ teaspoons lemon juice

Combine the cream cheese and butter. Slowly add the sugar, then vanilla and lemon juice. Whip until smooth.

Cherry Chocolate Layer Cake

It's not too sweet, and can be served with optional
frosting of choice, or the mock whipped cream and cherries.

1¾ cup Gluten-free All-Purpose flour blend
1 cup granulated sweetener
¾ cup cocoa powder
1½ teaspoons baking soda
1½ teaspoons baking powder
1 teaspoon salt
Egg Replacer for 2 eggs, prepared according to package
instructions
1 (21 ounce) can of Gluten-free cherry pie filling
1 teaspoon vanilla
¼ cup unsweetened applesauce
1 cup chocolate milk product, microwaved for 45 seconds
½ cup oil of choice
Mock whipped cream, optional

Preheat oven to 350°F. Grease a 9x13 inch pan.

Mix the flour, sugar, cocoa, baking soda, baking powder, prepared
Egg Replacer, and salt in a large mixing bowl. Mix in the pie filling,
applesauce, and oil. Add the warm milk, mixing gently. Pour into a
greased sheet cake and bake for about 30 minutes, until toothpick
comes out clean. Cool 30 minutes before serving.

Vegan Whipped Cream

16 Ounces Mimic Crème® or coconut milk
3 Tablespoons or more of liquid sweetener
2 teaspoons vanilla (use 4 teaspoons if using coconut milk)

Refrigerate cream overnight. Beat on high for 4 to 5 minutes until thickened. Stir in sweetener and vanilla. Beat mixture on high for an additional 10 to 15 minutes.

Place in the freezer until firm.

Use topping immediately or store it in the refrigerator for up to two days.

Spicy Bundt Cake with Chocolate Sauce

Preheat oven to 325°F.

Boil together, covered, for 3 minutes:
1 cup chai tea
2 cups raisins
1 cup brown sugar
½ cup coconut oil or vegan margarine
1 teaspoon cinnamon
½ teaspoon salt
¼ teaspoon ginger

Let cool while you mix together:
2 cups Gluten-free All-purpose flour
1 teaspoon baking powder
1 teaspoon baking soda
½ teaspoon Xanthan or Guar gum

Once blended, add liquid mixture. Pour batter into greased Bundt pan, and level with a spatula. Bake for one hour. Allow to cool completely before removing from the pan.

Chocolate Sauce
2/3 cup unsweetened cocoa
1 2/3 cups white sugar
1¼ cups water
1 teaspoon vanilla extract

In a medium saucepan over medium heat, combine cocoa, sugar and water. Bring to a boil and let boil 1 minute. Remove from heat and stir in vanilla.

Pineapple Upside Down Cake

Great cake to toss together last minute. Tastes awesome with non-dairy vanilla ice cream and some soy whip topping.

¼ cup oil
Egg Replacer for 3 eggs, prepared according to instructions
¼ teaspoon almond extract
Any brand of Gluten-free vegan cake mix
2/3 cup pineapple juice (reserved from pineapple rings)

Topping
¾ cup brown sugar
½ cup coconut oil
1 can pineapple slices in water (10 slices)
12 cherries without stems
Dairy-Free whipped topping, such as Soy Whip

Preheat oven to 325°F. Melt coconut oil in a 9-inch x 13-inch pan in oven. When melted, remove pan and sprinkle brown sugar over oil.

Place pineapple slices on bottom in a single layer. Place cherries in the centers of the pineapple rings. Whisk Egg Replacer in a large bowl until frothy. Add oil and whisk until incorporated. Add almond extract. Mix cake mix into the Egg Replacer mixture. Add pineapple juice.

Spoon cake mix evenly over pineapple rings and cherries, being careful not to make the rings move in the pan.

Bake for 25 to 30 minutes, or until toothpick inserted comes out clean. Let stand for 30 minutes, then invert cake onto plate.

Apple Bundt Cake

I exploded this cake, literally, by having too much leavening along with the Egg Replacer, which also has leavening. The pan has never been the same and my husband will never let me forget it. ☺

5 medium apples, room temperature, peeled, cored
¼ cup unsweetened applesauce
1 cup packed brown granulated sweetener
½ cup granulated sweetener
2 teaspoons vanilla extract
3 Tablespoons oil
¼ cup vegan sour cream
1 cup oat flour
1 cup almond meal/flour
¼ cup rice flour
½ cup cornstarch
1 ½ teaspoons baking powder
1 teaspoon baking soda
Egg Replacer for 2 eggs, prepared according to instructions
1 teaspoon Apple Pie Spice
1 teaspoon ground cinnamon
½ teaspoon salt
½ cup pecan or walnut halves

Preheat oven to 350°F.

Chop the apples and set aside.

In a separate bowl mix the Egg Replacer and add with the sugar until smooth. Add the vanilla, oil and sour cream; beat to combine.

Stir together the dry ingredients in a separate bowl. Slowly add them into the wet mixture and combine well.

Pour half of the cake batter into the prepared pan. Add the drained sugared apples into the batter. Add half of the nuts. Pour the remaining batter on top of the apples. Add the rest of the nuts to the top and lightly press in.

Bake in the center of a preheated oven for 1 hour, testing with a toothpick. If the cake begins to over-brown before it is done, cover the edges loosely with pieces of foil.

Orange Creamcicle Cake

Delicious on a hot day and for BBQ and other potlucks. Super moist.

2¼ cups all purpose Gluten-free flour
1 Tablespoon baking powder
½ teaspoon salt
1 ½ teaspoons Egg Replacer
1 teaspoon Xanthan or Guar gum
1¼ cups carbonated orange soda
3 Egg Replacer portions prepared according to instructions
1 cup granulated sweetener
2 teaspoons grated orange zest
1 stick (8 Tablespoons or 4 ounces) vegan butter
½ teaspoon orange extract
½ teaspoon vanilla
1 cup fresh squeezed orange juice

For the frosting:
3 Tablespoons rice flour
1 cup milk product
¾ cup vegan butter
1 teaspoon orange extract
1 teaspoon vanilla extract
2/3 cup granulated sweetener
2/3 cup orange marmalade, optional

Preheat oven to 350°F. Grease a 9x13 cake pan and line and set aside.

Sift together the flour, baking powder, salt, and gum.

Whisk together the Egg Replacer in a small bowl.

Put the sweetener and orange zest in a mixer bowl and beat with the butter until you have a nice, creamy texture. Add Egg Replacer to the mixture and beat again until thoroughly combined. Remove the mixer bowl from the stand and gently fold in the soda.

Slowly sift flour mixture into the bowl, folding in after 1/3 of the flour has been added. Add another 1/3 of the flour mixture, fold, and add the rest, folding until you have a nice cake texture. Add up to ¼ cup unsweetened applesauce if the batter seems dry.

Divide the batter between the two pans and smooth the tops with a rubber spatula.

Bake for 30-35 minutes, or until a toothpick comes out clean. Transfer the cakes to cooling racks and cool for about 5 minutes, then run a knife around the sides of the cakes, unfold them and peel off the paper liners.

When cake has cooled, poke holes in the top with a fork. Pour orange juice over tops of cake.

Frost and keep refrigerated.

Vanilla Cake with Mocha Frosting

This was by far the hardest recipe to make, as I was unsuccessful in creating a layer cake that would not cave in, slip off the bottom layer, or crack in half.

1 cup sorghum flour
1 cup rice flour
2 cups cornstarch
2 cups granulated sweetener
1 teaspoon salt
2 teaspoons baking powder
2 teaspoons baking soda
2 teaspoon Xanthan or Guar gum
2 cups warm milk product
2 Tablespoons Egg Replacer made with ½ cup warm water
½ cup oil
2 Tablespoons vanilla
½ teaspoon lemon juice

Preheat oven to 350°F.

Combine all ingredients and use an electric mixer to blend well for 2-3 minutes. Divide equally into 2 round greased cake pans or one large 13x9 pan. Bake 20-25 minutes, or until the tops turn golden and a toothpick comes out clean. I suggest frosting with the Mocha Frosting on the next page.

Mocha Frosting

4 cups confectioner's sugar
4 Tablespoons cocoa powder
½ cup vegan shortening
½ cup cold coffee, or coffee flavored milk product
1 Tablespoon vanilla

Cream shortening and sugar together until thick. Gradually stir in coffee/milk product, then vanilla.

To finish, blend in the cocoa powder.

Refrigerate 1 hour to set before using.

Cookies,
Brownies,
&
Bars

Banana Nut Oat Cookies

Makes 3 dozen

3 cups oat flour
1 teaspoon of baking powder
1 teaspoon salt product
1 cup granulated sweetener or ¾ cup liquid sweetener
2 teaspoons of oil
2/3 cup milk product
2 mashed bananas
2 teaspoons vanilla
2/3 cup raisins, soaked in ½ cup hot water, optional

Preheat oven to 350° F.

Combine all wet ingredients in one bowl and all dry ingredients in the other. Slowly fold the dry into the wet and stir well. When done, add optional raisins and gently fold into the batter. Grease cookie sheets. Spoon batter onto sheets in rounded teaspoonfuls, 1 inch apart.

Bake for 6 minutes, rotate pans, and bake 4-6 minutes until the edges begin to turn golden.

Let cool on sheets 5 minutes before transferring to a wire rack.

Homemade Grahams

These cookies are great for your own cracker crumbs for pies, cheesecakes, etc. They are of course equally good eaten alone, with jelly, or frosting.

Makes 6 Dozen

2¼ cups Gluten-free All-Purpose flour
½ cup packed brown sweetener
2 teaspoons cinnamon
1 teaspoon baking powder
½ teaspoon Xanthan or Guar gum
½ teaspoon baking soda
½ teaspoon salt or salt substitute
½ cup vegan butter
3 Tablespoons cold water
3 Tablespoons liquid sweetener
2 teaspoon vanilla

Mix together flour, brown sweetener, cinnamon, baking powder, Xanthan gum, baking soda, and salt. Work butter into dry ingredients. Stir in 3 Tablespoons cold water, liquid sweetener, and vanilla. If dough is too dry, add a small amount of water. Gather dough into a soft ball. Refrigerate for an hour.

Preheat oven to 325°F.

Roll a piece of dough on a floured surface to about 1/8-inch thickness. Cut into 2 x 3-inch pieces and prick lightly all over with a fork. Take remaining sheet with dough on it and turn it over. Lay it flat, rolled dough side down, onto prepared pan. Bake for 12 to 15 minutes or until golden brown.

Blondies

I suggest popping any leftovers in the microwave to serve warm.

1½ cups Gluten-free All-purpose flour
¼ cup Gluten-free rolled oats or Quinoa flakes
¾ cup brown sweetener
1 teaspoon baking powder
1 teaspoon cinnamon
½ cup vegetable oil
½ cup unsweetened applesauce
1 portion of Egg Replacer, prepared according to package
1 ½ teaspoons vanilla
¼ cup chocolate chips
½ cup nuts (I use Macadamia)

Preheat the oven to 350°F.

Make the Egg Replacer and set aside.

Mix the dry ingredients together in a large bowl. Add the oil, applesauce, vanilla, and Egg Replacer . Mix until all ingredients are fully incorporated. Add the chocolate chips and walnuts.

Pour into a greased 8" x 8" baking dish. If you have some extra chips or
walnuts sprinkle them on top to decorate the blondies.

Bake for 25-30 minutes. Allow to cool for 15 minutes before cutting.

Buttery Shortbread Cookies

These, along with my crumb cake, were my signature recipe, and therefore one of the first for my Gluten-free vegan conversion.

2 Dozen

1½ cups confectioner's sugar
1 cup vegan shortening
1½ teaspoons Egg Replacer, prepared according to instructions
2 teaspoons vanilla
2½ cups Gluten-free All-purpose flour
½ teaspoon Xanthan or Guar gum
1 teaspoon baking soda
1 teaspoon cream of tartar

Place confectioner's sugar and shortening in the bowl of an electric mixer and beat on medium speed until smooth and slightly fluffy. Add Egg Replacer and vanilla. Mix well.

In a separate bowl, combine flour mix, gum, baking soda and cream of tartar. Add flour to sugar mixture, beating on low speed until thoroughly combined. Gather dough into a ball and chill for 2 hours.

Preheat oven to 350°F.

Lightly flour your work surface and rolling pin. Roll out dough to ¼ inch thickness and cut into shapes with cookie cutters or simply place spoonfuls of dough onto sheets. Transfer cookies to cookie greased sheets.

Bake cookies on center rack for 10 minutes, rotating sheets after 5 minutes.

Peanut Butter Oatmeal Chocolate Chip Cookies

My husband's favorite cookie, other than Snickerdoodles.

2 dozen

    1¼ cups Gluten-free All-purpose flour
    4 teaspoons flaxseed meal
    1 cup Gluten-free rolled oats or Quinoa flakes
    1 cup brown sweetener
    2 teaspoons baking powder
    1 teaspoon baking soda
    ½ teaspoon sea salt
    1 teaspoon Xanthan or Guar gum
    1 teaspoon vanilla
    ¼ cup oil
    ½ cup liquid sweetener
    ¾ cup chunky peanut butter
    1 bag of vegan chocolate chips

Preheat oven to 350°F.

Mix all the ingredients in a large bowl, stirring well to incorporate everything together.

Drop the dough onto either a greased cookie sheet. My husband likes when I put fork lines in them.

Bake 6 minutes, rotate pans, and bake another 4-6 minutes, until they are just becoming crisp around the edges.

Coconut Macaroons

I find this recipe really pops when you use coconut flour, but you
certainly can use Gluten-free All-purpose flour instead.

2 Egg Replacer portions, prepared according to instructions
6 Tablespoons coconut milk or water
½ cup granulated sweetener
1 Tablespoon arrowroot or cornstarch
1 dash salt
½ cup coconut flour
2 cups shredded coconut
1 teaspoon baking powder

Preheat oven to at 325°F.

Mix Egg Replacer and water according to package instructions. Add
next 4 ingredients and gently stir to combine. Stir in coconut just
enough to mix. If needed, add a little water if the dough is too stiff to
work with. Form into small balls and drop into lightly oiled baking
sheet.

Bake 15-20 minutes or until the macaroons begin to turn golden.
You will have to carefully watch these if you are using another shape
other than the round we used in our recipe to Guard from over
baking.

Cool 10 minutes on cookie sheets before transferring to wire rack.

Chewy Fig Cookies

Like Newtons and easier to make than you might think.

Filling

1 pack of cut up dried figs
1 cup water

Fig Directions

Soak overnight and/or simmer until soft and process until smooth.

Dough Ingredients

1 cup coconut oil
1/3 cup liquid sweetener
1 teaspoon vanilla
½ teaspoon baking soda
1½ cups brown rice flour
2 teaspoons Xanthan or Guar gum
½ teaspoon salt

Preheat oven to 350°F.

 Combine cookie dough ingredients in food processor until they form a ball, then roll out half of the dough (or press) into a pie pan or cake pan for the bottom layer.

Next, spread the fig filling on the layer and roll out the rest of the dough for top of the crust between two pieces of Gluten-free floured wax paper for easy handling. Flip on top of fig filling and bake for about 12-15 minutes until light brown.

Snickerdoodles

½ cup coconut oil or vegan shortening
¾ cup granulated sweetener
Egg Replacer for one egg, prepared according to instructions
2 teaspoons vanilla
½ cup tapioca starch
¾ cup potato starch
¼ teaspoon baking soda
1 teaspoon baking powder
1 teaspoon Xanthan or Guar gum
½ teaspoon salt
2 Tablespoons milk product
2 Tablespoons granulated sweetener mixed with ½ teaspoon cinnamon
½ teaspoon cream of tartar

Preheat oven to 350°F.

In a large bowl, cream together coconut oil/shortening and sugar. Add Egg Replacer and vanilla. Mix well.

Add potato starch, tapioca, baking soda, cream of tartar, baking powder, gum, salt, and milk. Mix well. Dough will be sticky.

Lightly oil hands and any tools you may use to work with dough. Shape into small balls, using a slightly-rounded teaspoon of dough for each cookie. Submerge each cookie into the cinnamon sugar mix.

Bake for 12 minutes, rotating the sheets after 6 minutes.

Hot Fudge Brownies

Makes two 9x9 pans

2 cups Gluten-free All-purpose flour
½ cup granulated sweetener
¾ cup powdered cocoa
4 Tablespoons baking powder
1 teaspoon salt product
1 cup chocolate milk product
¼ cup oil
1 Tablespoon vanilla extract
3½ cups boiling hot water, divided
2 cups packed brown granulated sweetener

Preheat oven to 350°F.

In large bowl, combine flour, white sugar, 4 teaspoons cocoa, baking powder and salt. Stir in milk, oil, and vanilla until smooth.

Spread into two 9x9 square baking pans. Combine brown sweetener and remaining cocoa into a separate bowl until blended, then sprinkle over the two pans equally.

Pour 1¾ cup hot water over each pan. For hot fudge effect, do not stir.

Bake for 35-40 minutes until toothpicks come out clean. Rotate pans after 20 minutes.

Best served warm with mock whipped cream or non-dairy ice cream.

Oreo-Style Sandwiches

I make these really large and wrap them up for Christmas. Feel free
to dress them up with spinkles, chocolate chips, or other stir ins.

1¼ cup Gluten-free All-purpose Flour
½ cup unsweetened cocoa
1½ teaspoons Xanthan or Guar gum
1 teaspoon baking soda
¼ teaspoon baking powder
¼ teaspoon salt
1 cup granulated sweetener
½ cup plus 2 Tablespoons vegan butter, room temperature
Egg Replacer for one egg, prepared according to
instructions

Preheat oven to 350°F.

Mix the flour, cocoa, gum, baking soda and powder, salt, and sugar.
Beat in the butter and the Egg Replacer. Continue mixing until
dough comes together.

Take rounded teaspoons of batter and place on a greased cookie
sheet approximately 2 inches apart.

Bake for 9 minutes at 350°F. Allow to fully cool before making
sandwiches with your favorite frosting.

Lemon Bars

Crust Ingredients
½ cup vegan butter, at room temperature
¼ cup confectioners' sugar
1 cup Gluten-free All-purpose flour
1 teaspoon of Xanthan or Guar gum

Filling Ingredients
½ cup silken tofu (soft preferred)
1 cup granulated sweetener
Zest from 2 lemons
1/3 cup fresh lemon juice
2 Tablespoons Gluten-free All-purpose flour
1 cup confectioners' sugar, sifted

Preheat the oven to 350°F.

Grease an 8 x 8 baking pan with oil (or use a cooking spray) and sprinkle with just a light dusting of flour. To make the crust, cream the butter and confectioners' sugar with an electric mixer until light and fluffy. Add the flour, and beat until the dough just comes together.

Press the crust into the bottom of your pan and bake for 20 minutes, or until lightly browned. Blend the tofu in a food processor or blender until creamy. Add the sweetener to the tofu, and blend until smooth. Blend in the lemon zest, lemon juice, flour, and starch.

Pour the filling over the crust and bake for about 20 minutes, or until the filling is set. Remove from the oven and cool. The bars will set as they cool. To serve, cut into squares or bars and dust with sifted confectioners' sugar.

Chocolate Biscotti

When I was in the midst of writing this book, I asked a good friend of mine, Gerren, what type of recipe he would like for me to try. Without hesitation, he said "Chocolate Biscotti". He has since moved out of the area, so I was unable to have him try the finished product. However, I do believe he would give his seal of approval.

1 cup millet flour
2/3 cup buckwheat flour
1/3 quinoa flour
½ cup unsweetened cocoa
1½ teaspoons baking soda
1 teaspoon salt
1½ teaspoons ground cinnamon
A pinch of nutmeg
1 teaspoon Xanthan or Guar gum
½ cup chopped pecans or walnuts, if desired

In a separate bowl, blend:
½ cup vegan shortening
2/3 cup agave nectar (syrups do not work as well)
1/3 cup almond or other nut butter
1 Tablespoon vanilla
Egg Replacer for 2 large eggs, prepared according to package

Preheat oven to 350° F. Line a baking sheet with parchment.

Mix all ingredients as directed above in separate bowls, then combine. The dough will be quite hard to stir, so use your hands. If the dough is too dry, add a Tablespoon of milk or water until the dough holds together.

Place dough on to the baking sheet and press to make a log shape that you want the biscotti to be.

Bake the dough in the center of a preheated oven for 20 to 30 minutes, or
until the dough is firm and be dry in the center. Let cool for at least 20 minutes.

Reduce oven to 300° F.

When the dough is cool enough to handle, slice it crosswise. Lay the biscotti on the parchment and bake them for 10 to 12 minutes or so until crisp.

Ginger Cream Sandwiches

This combination was discovered when I was perfecting my vanilla frosting recipe. I grabbed one of my ginger cookies and dipped it in. The combination of sweet and sharp won me over, and I bet it will for you, too.

2 Dozen

2 cups Gluten-free All-purpose flour
2 cups oat flour or other gluten-free flour of choice
2 cups granulated sweetener
1 cup brown granulated sweetener
2/3 cup unsweetened applesauce
1½ cups oil
2 teaspoons salt
1/3 cup molasses
4 Tablespoons vanilla
¼ cup flaxseed meal
Egg Replacer for 2 eggs prepared according to instructions
2 Tablespoons cinnamon
2 Tablespoons ginger
2 teaspoons baking soda
2 teaspoons Xanthan or Guar gum
Vanilla frosting to make sandwiches, if desired

Preheat oven to 350°F.

Grease cookie sheets. In a bowl, add all dry ingredients. Add oil, applesauce, vanilla, and molasses.

Drop Tablespoon sized portions of batter on cookie sheets. Bake 8 minutes, rotate pans, and bake another 5 minutes, until they begin to brown. Allow cookies to cool about 30 minutes, before making into sandwiches.

Pies
&
Fruit
Desserts

Pie Crust

This was by far my hardest creation, as I had never actually made traditional pie crust. Every combination of flours I tried was horrible. Then, when I was about done trying, this happened!

Makes 2 Crusts

1½ cups all purpose Gluten-free flour
½ cup brown rice flour
½ cup garbanzo bean flour
2teaspoons Xanthan or Guar gum
1 teaspoon salt
1 teaspoon of granulated sweetener
½ cup vegan butter or shortening
½ cup ice water

Mix flours, gum, sugar, and salt in a large bowl; add the butter or shortening, and use a pastry blender to blend until the mixture resembles coarse meal.

Add ice water slowly, while gently stirring with a spatula just until dough holds together without being wet or sticky. You may not need the full ½ cup portion, and you will find that the amount varies every time you make this recipe. Do not over-knead the dough. To test, squeeze a small amount together: If it is crumbly, add more ice water, 1 Tablespoon at a time.

Form dough into a ball. Flatten into a disc and wrap in plastic. Transfer to the refrigerator and chill at least 1 hour before using.

Apple Pie

Who doesn't like Apple pie on Thanksgiving?

2 Prepared pie crusts
¾ cup granulated sweetener
2 Tablespoons oat or other Gluten-free flour
1 teaspoon ground cinnamon
1 to 2 teaspoons lemon juice
6 cups thinly sliced, peeled and cored granny apples
1 Tablespoon vegan butter
Milk product of choice (for glazing)

Put one crust in bottom of 9 inch pie plate. In small bowl, combine sugar and next 4 ingredients. Place half of thinly sliced apples in piecrust; sprinkle with half of sugar mixture. Top with rest of apples, then rest of sugar mixture. Dot the filling with margarine.

Preheat oven to 425° F.

Roll out remaining crust. Cut out a design or make slits in top using a
knife. Place crust over pie; trim edges. Fold pastry overhang under then bring up over pie plate rim. Pinch to form a high edge then make your choice of decorative edge.

For golden glaze, brush the top crust (not the edge) lightly with some soy or rice milk.

Bake pie for 40-50 minutes or until crust is golden.

Pecan Pie

(1) Already prepared pie crust (for bottom only)
1 ¼ cups of pecan halves
½ cup brown granulated sweetener
¾ cup granulated sweetener
1½ cups regular or sugar-free maple syrup
1 teaspoon vanilla
¾ cup milk product
¼ cup cornstarch
½ cup water or bourbon
2 Tablespoons vegan butter, melted
1 teaspoon salt

Preheat oven to 400°F.

Grease a pie pan and place one crust in the bottom. Poke holes with a fork, and pre-bake crust for 10 minutes. While baking, prepare the pie filling.

In a medium saucepan combine the water, sweetener, and the maple syrup. Bring to a boil and boil for 5 minutes. Dissolve cornstarch in the water. Add the salt and the dissolved cornstarch to the pot, whisking vigorously.

Stir and cook over high heat just until the mixture thickens and is clear. Remove from heat and stir in the pecans, margarine, and vanilla. Let cool for a few minutes. The mixture will still be fairly liquid. Pour this into the pre-baked pie shell.

Reduce the heat to 350°F. Bake 30 minutes. The filling may seem undercoooked, but it will solidify as it cools. Cool on a rack for about 1 ½ hours, then refrigerate until thoroughly cooled and set.

Dutch Cherry Pie

I must confess that I make this just to eat the crumb. After all,
is there such a thing as just crumb pie?

1 can of cherry filling or topping
1 unbaked pie crust for bottom
Lemon juice
1 cup Gluten-free rolled oats or quinoa flakes
½ cup Gluten-free All-Purpose flour
2/3 cup brown granulated sweetener
6 Tablespoons vegan butter
1 teaspoon vanilla
½ teaspoon cinnamon

Preheat the oven to 375°F.

Mix the can of cherries with the lemon (use enough to make it tart,
but not too sour). Pour filling in unbaked shell.

Blend the oats/quinoa, brown sweetener, flour, butter, cinnamon,
vanilla on low speed until it forms a coarse meal.

Crumble the mixture evenly over the cherry pie filling and sprinkle
with a bit more lemon juice, if desired.

Bake for 40 minutes.

Blueberry Cobbler

You can use a mix of blueberries and raspberries when they are in season.

  1 pint fresh organic blueberries
  ½ cup sorghum flour
  ½ teaspoon salt
  ½ teaspoon Xanthan or Guar gum
  ½ teaspoon baking soda
  1 ½ teaspoons baking powder
  1 teaspoon cinnamon
  3-4 Tablespoons liquid sweetener
  3-4 Tablespoons oil
  ½ cup vanilla milk product
  1 teaspoon vanilla

Preheat oven to 350°F.

Lightly oil an 8x8-inch baking dish. Pour the blueberries into the prepared baking dish.

In a mixing bowl, combine the dry ingredients with a whisk. Combine the wet ingredients in a large measuring cup and pour into the dry mix.

Stir together to form a batter. If the batter appears too dry, add more a little more liquid one spoonful at a time.

Drop topping by hefty spoonfuls onto the blueberries. Bake 20-35 minutes, until topping is brown and fruit is bubbly underneath. This cobbler is best eaten warm with non-dairy ice cream on top.

Triple Berry Crisp

4 cups assorted berries, fresh or frozen
3/4 cup granulated sweetener
3 Tablespoons tapioca
¼ teaspoon cinnamon
¾ cup water
1 Tablespoon lemon juice
1 cup Gluten-free All-Purpose flour
2 Tablespoon granulated sweetener of choice
1½ teaspoons baking powder
¼ teaspoon salt
2 Tablespoons vegan butter
½ cup milk product

Preheat oven to 350°F.

Grease a 9-inch square baking pan, spoon the fruit into it, and set aside.

Whisk together the sweetener, tapioca, and the cinnamon in a saucepan. Add the water and the lemon juice, and bring to a boil over medium-high heat. When the mixture is bubbly, pour it over the berries in the baking pan, and set aside.

In a mixing bowl, combine the flour, 2 Tablespoons of sweetener, baking powder, and salt. Cut in the butter until the mixture consists of coarse crumbs. Pour in the milk and stir with a fork until the dough clings together. Drop chunks of the dough by heaping Tablespoonfuls onto the fruit mixture, until all the dough has been used.

Bake for about 30 minutes, or until the topping is golden brown.

Miscellaneous Treats

Peanut Butter Candy Bars

I am personally addicted to these, and hold them personally responsible for a bit of weight I gained in the course of writing this book ☺

1 cup vegan butter, melted
2 cups our graham crackers crushed, or other cookie crumbs
2 cups confectioner's sugar
1 cup peanut butter
1½ cups vegan chocolate chips
4 Tablespoons peanut butter

In a medium bowl, mix together the butter, graham cracker crumbs, confectioners' sugar, and 1 cup peanut butter until well blended.

Press evenly into the bottom of an ungreased 9x13 inch pan. In a metal bowl over simmering water, or in the microwave, melt the chocolate chips with the peanut butter, stirring occasionally until smooth. Spread over the prepared crust.

Refrigerate for at least one hour before cutting into squares.

Peanut Butter Fudge

Another delicious no-bake treat. Great for holidays and parties.

¾ cup vegan butter
1 cup peanut butter
3 cups confectioners' sugar
2/3 cup cocoa powder

Lightly grease a 9x9 inch baking dish.

In a saucepan over low heat, melt butter. Remove from heat and stir in peanut butter until smooth.

Stir in confectioners' sugar, a little at a time, until well blended. Pat into prepared pan and chill until firm. Cut into squares.

Chocolate Nut Truffles

You can use any nuts of choice, but I prefer it best with cashews.

¾ cup raw cashews
¾ cup cold water
1 pound of vegan bittersweet chocolate
Cocoa powder to roll truffles in

Put cashews and cold water in a blender and blend at high speed for 1-2 minutes. Scrape the sides and blend again until the mixture is thick and frothy.

Meanwhile, in a double boiler heat the chocolate until melted. Cool until it's comfortable to work with and fold in the cashew cream.

Refrigerate for at least two hours.

Remove from refrigerator and form into small balls. Roll balls in cocoa powder. Chill and serve.

Chocolate Pudding

I have fooled many unsuspecting eaters into eating tofu with this recipe.

1 box silken tofu
¼ cup cocoa powder
1 teaspoon vanilla
Dash salt
¼ cup sweetener of choice

Blend all ingredients in food processor until smooth. Let chill in the refrigerator for at least 1 hour.

Sweet Cereal Party Mix

There are a number of Gluten-free vegan cereals on the market, so choose your favorite.

9 cups Gluten-free vegan cereal
2 cups shredded coconut
1 cup peanuts or other nuts
1 cup packed light brown granulated sweetener
½ cup (1 stick) vegan butter
½ cup liquid sweetener
1 teaspoon vanilla extract
½ teaspoon baking soda
1 bag of vegan chocolate chips
1 ½ cups raisins

Preheat oven to 250°F.

Combine cereal, coconut and nuts in a large baking pan. In small saucepan over medium heat, heat brown sweetener, butter and liquid sweetener t boiling.

Lower and simmer for 5 minutes. Stir in vanilla and baking soda.

Pour over cereal mixture, stir until evenly coated.

Bake 1 hour, stirring every 15 minutes. Cool, stirring frequently. Stir in chocolate and raisins.

When cool, sprinkle with optional confectioners' sugar.

Featured Products

Ener-g Egg Replacer www.ener-g.com

Bob's Gluten-free Flours www.bobsredmill.com

Now Foods www.nowfoods.com

Jules Gluten-free flour www.julesglutenfree.com

Barry Farms Gluten-free flours www.barryfarms.com

Earth Balance www.earthbalancenatural.com

About the Author

Dawn Grey, PhD, is a Certified Holistic Health Practitioner and owner of the Aruna Center of Lawrence, Kansas. After discovering her lifelong health issues were the results of dairy, egg, and gluten sensitivities in 2001, she changed her diet and the scope of her consultation business to help others identify and manage their own sensitivities. Now, eight years later, she is healthier, leaner, and happier than ever before.

Dawn is available for personal wellness coaching by special appointment. For more information about being a distance client of the Aruna Center, please contact Dawn at reikirays@yahoo.com

For additional holistic and metaphysical services, please visit her website at www.arunacenter.com

In addition to this book, Dawn is the author of six other cookbooks for vegan and gluten-free audiences, a tarot book "Reading the Tarot", and "The Complete Usui Reiki Master Manual".

For those interested in learning more about holistic and natural methods of health and healing, Dawn and her staff over accredited distance education courses at www.reikiraysinstitute.com

Visit our site, www.newdawnkitchen.com for pictures of all of our recipes in this book, as well as additions and information on upcoming books in the series.

Made in the USA
Lexington, KY
10 April 2011